Tiny Bubbles

Tiny Bubbles

Fizzy Cocktails for Every Occasion,
Using Champagne, Prosecco, and Other Sparkling Wines

By Kate Simon
Photographs by Sheri Giblin

CHRONICLE BOOKS
SAN FRANCISCO

Library of Congress Cataloging-in-Publication Data available.

ISBN 978-0-8118-6226-4

Manufactured in China.

Design by **Vanessa Dina**

Prop styling by **spork**

Food styling by **spork**

Typesetting by **Janis Reed**

The stylist wishes to thank La Maison for the spoons on page 86.

Blendtec is a copyright of K-TEC, Inc.
Creamsicle is a copyright of Unilever.
Popsicle is a copyright of Unilever.

10 9 8 7 6 5 4 3 2 1
Chronicle Books LLC
680 Second Street
San Francisco, California 94107
www.chroniclebooks.com

ACKNOWLEDGMENTS

Here's to the early cocktailians with the foresight to
write down their recipes, and to the contemporary drink
historians who rediscovered the classic tipples.

Big thanks to Mark Rutherford, Lori Millbauer,
Audra Rutherford, and all the friends who selflessly lent their
palates to this project. Thanks also to Karen Foley and the rest
of the *Imbibe* staff, for the inspiration; Jennifer Tomaro,
Bill LeBlond, and Amy Treadwell at Chronicle Books; my agent,
Faye Bender; Ariel Gore; and Jeanne Sather.

| CONTENTS |

Bubbly cocktails are the most festive drinks of all time.

They never go out of style. Even in the last few decades of the twentieth century—a dismal era in the proud history of the cocktail—people still managed to sip Mimosas with brunch and cobble together sugar cubes, bitters, and Champagne on New Year's Eves. When a bottle of bubbly is popped at a gathering, something magical happens: It becomes a celebration. And when that Champagne is mixed ceremoniously with other ingredients, like imported liqueurs or fresh fruits and herbs, now we're really partying.

Classic and classic-inspired cocktails are back in a big way. Bubbly concoctions never went away, but they're being revisited and reimagined. Some bar chefs are elevating sparklers by adding culinary-inspired fresh ingredients, digging through nineteenth-century cocktail books to riff off old-time recipes, and looking to Italy and other parts of Europe where fizzy cocktails are a part of everyday life. Those who like their cocktails simple and easy—pour juice in glass, add sparkling wine, and clink with your neighbor—are exploring variations on the Mimosa and the Bellini, embellishing the old standards with updated ingredients like hand-squeezed clementine juice, apricot purée, and fresh herbs.

The bubbly itself has been updated, too. While Champagne is still an excellent, undeniably stylish choice, its price tag can be as big as its good reputation. Luckily, other sparkling wines can be just as delicious in cocktails. They all have their own personalities, from California's Champagne-style sparkling wines to Italy's supple Prosecco, Spain's fruity cava, Australia's head-turning sparkling reds, and Japan's sparkling sake. These national treasures, some the product of longtime tradition and some more current innovations, are quickly earning appreciation for their mixability.

Bubbly cocktails aren't just for New Year's Eve anymore. In parts of Europe, sparklers are popular as everyday predinner aperitifs—the tongue-tingling effervescence preps the palate for a meal. Fizzy cocktails will always be a hit at weddings, anniversaries, and other fancy fetes, but don't save them for a special occasion; they're also crowd-pleasers at brunches, lunches, and backyard barbecues. As Lucius Beebe noted in his 1946 classic *The Stork Club Bar Book*, "Champagne is practically the only wine that lends itself to absorption twenty-four hours around the clock."

So have a Bellini with breakfast, and for dinner, raise a French 75 to celebrate the pizza being delivered on time. Here's to prosciutto, fresh basil, and extra mozzarella!

CHAPTER 1

Sparkling Wine Guide

There's more to sparkling wine than Champagne. In addition to the iconic French sparkler, the recipes in this book call for a range of sparkling wines from all over the world. This chapter's cheat sheets on choosing and using bubbly—including tips on opening the intimidating bottles—will help you maintain your dignity in your dealings with the showy wine.

Choosing a Bubbly

Many sparkling wines are interchangeable, but they all have their own quirks and qualities. Here's a guide to the wines recommended in this book.

ASTI: A somewhat sweet, fruity, moderately sparkling Italian wine made from Muscat grapes. At its best, it can taste like ripe peaches and crisp white grapes.

CAVA: A Spanish sparkling wine similar to Champagne. It can be fruity, earthy, and very bubbly, with crisp apple notes. A good substitute for Champagne, at a good value.

CHAMPAGNE: A fully sparkling wine made in the Champagne region of France according to a strict tradition called the *méthode champenoise*. It can be earthy, pungent, and complex, with notes of apple and stone fruits.

MOSCATO D'ASTI: A sweet, mildly sparkling Italian wine made from the Muscat grape. It can have a gorgeously floral, fruity flavor and aroma. Think honeysuckle.

PROSECCO: A moderately sparkling Italian wine with a supple body and hints of apple and peach. Its softness and low alcohol content make it a versatile mixer. It's much milder than Champagne.

SEKT: A fully sparkling German wine that's been improving in quality in recent years. The best are made from Riesling grapes and can be fruity and dry or slightly sweet.

SPARKLING RED: Lightly sparkling red wine, usually from Australia—notable examples are sparkling Shiraz and Cabernet—or Italy, as in its sparkling Lambrusco. Deep purple in color with crimson fizz, it can express bold flavors of oak, berries, and spices. It's unexpected and fun, but not a match for every cocktail.

SPARKLING ROSÉ: A pink Champagne or other sparkling wine that usually gets its color from red grapes with the skins left on. At their best, rosés are crisp and fruity and not overly dry or sweet, with a light flavor and color that make them alluring in cocktails.

SPARKLING SAKE: A gently sparkling sake (a fermented, mildly alcoholic Japanese beverage made from rice) with a milky white color. It can be lightly spicy and very fruity, with notes of melon.

SPARKLING WINE: All sparkling wines fall into this category, but in this book, I use the term to refer to Champagne-style sparklers made *outside* the Champagne region, in California and other U.S. states, Australia, New Zealand, South Africa, France, Chile, Argentina, Canada, and, increasingly, other parts of the world. These can be earthy and very fruity, with notes of stone fruits, apples, and bananas. Many of them are good substitutes for Champagne, most notably California sparkling wines made with Chardonnay and sometimes labeled "Champagne-style" or "blanc de blancs."

How Sweet It Is

Sparkling wines come in a range of dryness, from joltingly bone-dry to dessert sweet. The sparklers suitable for most of the cocktails in this book are either *brut* (very dry) or *extra dry* (slightly sweeter, but still on the dry side). In each recipe, the ideal level of dryness is indicated. Some bubblies, like sparkling sake, sparkling red, Asti, and Moscato d'Asti are listed without dryness indicators because they are not typically labeled or sold that way.

Open Sesame

Popping a bottle of bubbly doesn't have to be loud, explosive, messy, or danger-ous. (Though you should always be careful, and point the cork away from people or breakables.) The pop should really sound more like a light "poof," and the contents of the bottle should remain safely inside. The really easy way to do this is to invest in a cork-popping tool like Screwpull's Cork Catcher or Metrokane's Velvet Champagne Pliers. Both take the "scary" out of sparkling wine by catching the cork before it has time to do any damage. I like the peace of mind and predictable result I get from my Screwpull, but tools aren't crucial. All you really need is a dish towel (and after some practice, you might not even need that).

1.

Be sure the bottle is well chilled. (An hour in the refrigerator should do the trick.) Room-temperature bubbly can (and probably will) send foam flying when it's opened.

2.

Keeping the bottle pointed away from people or breakables, remove the wire cage from the cork.

3.

Drape a clean dish towel over the cork and wrap one hand around it, gripping the cork firmly.

4.

Holding the cork stationary, use your other hand to turn the bottle slowly in a counterclockwise direction. Be patient. Keep turning. The cork should come out with a "poof," safely into your towel-lined hand.

5.

Repeat often. Practice makes perfect.

Some bottles, like Prosecco, sake, and others that are only mildly sparkling, don't have fancy Champagne-style corks at all. For those, a wine opener or even a bottle opener might suffice. Increasingly, even fully sparkling wines are being released with crown caps (think vintage soda or beer bottles), a closure that's traditionally used during the Champagne production process before the fancy corks and wire cages are put on.

Storing Bubbly

The jury's still out on whether sparklers are best stored upright or horizontally. One sure thing is that if you put an opened bottle back in the fridge, a champagne saver is a must. Vacuvin makes a heavy-duty one that keeps the bubbles fresh for a week and lets you pour subsequent servings of champagne without removing the stopper. Argyle's lockable stopper, Sur La Table's clamp-style version, and the simple lever-style bottle stoppers that sell for less than $2 all work well, holding the fizz and the flavor for several days.

Glassware

Traditionally, Champagne was served in a round, wide-mouthed *coupe*, or saucer, which is rumored to have been modeled after Marie Antoinette's breast. Contemporary bubbly enthusiasts favor the taller, narrower flute because it preserves the fizz longer. But when the prolonged fizz factor isn't an issue, I prefer the classic look of saucers. They're also sturdier than flutes, and I like a good solid glass. I think of the saucer as an all-purpose vessel, suitable for any recipe that calls for a cocktail glass (the Martini kind), bubbly or not. Many of the recipes in this book call simply for a "sparkling-wine glass," which means either a saucer or a flute would work well. Others call specifically for a flute, such as when the presentation depends on the extra bubbles this glass shape yields. There are five main types of glassware recommended in this book:

CORDIAL GLASS:
Short and sweet,
2 ounces

HIGHBALL:
For drinks served over
ice, 10 ounces

GOBLET:
Big round bowl,
8 to 10 ounces

PUNCH GLASS:
Just like Grannie's, 4 ounces

SPARKLING-WINE GLASS:
Saucer (coupe) or flute, 6 ounces

Of course, you can use any old glass you please, but these libations deserve a pretty vessel, and if you choose one bigger than the recommended glass, be sure to alter the drink proportions appropriately.

When in doubt, chill the glass—and the ingredients. In Charles H. Baker Jr.'s 1939 classic, *The Gentleman's Companion, Vol. II*, the world-traveling gourmand insisted that his Champagne glasses be chilled, stating, "Warm Champagne is a foetid thing, of brassy taste, astringent to the throat, an insult to the nostrils." When cocktail ingredients are shaken with ice, chilled glasses aren't necessary, but many sparkling cocktails are built in the glass, without shaking. In these cases, it's important to use chilled bubbly—and chilled glasses are a nice touch, too, lest we offend our nostrils.

To chill a glass, place it in the refrigerator for at least 1 hour, or fill it with ice cubes and cold water, let sit for 15 minutes, then dump the ice water out, shaking out any remaining water before building the cocktail. Pre-Prohibition bartenders often added a lump of ice to the glass when mixing an unshaken cocktail, to both cool and dilute the drink. This is still an option for drinks built in the glass, like the Champagne Cocktail (page 16), but be sure not to overdilute.

CHAPTER 2

Classics

Ever since Champagne came into vogue in the eighteenth century, bartenders have been experimenting with the stuff. Classic sparkling cocktails ranged from the simple, chic Champagne cocktail, which is essentially an embellished glass of Champagne, to more ornate concoctions like the rich, almond-kissed Crimean Cup à la Marmora (page 36). Two-ingredient cocktails like the beloved Mimosa and Bellini—part juice, part sparkling wine—occupy a corner of their own in the bubbly Hall of Fame. The fourteen classics compiled here represent a range of styles and schools of thought, from a beer cocktail to a pastis-based drink meant for midday tippling to a couple of decorative punches. That these recipes are printed here at all is owed to the artistry of pre-Prohibition bartenders and the diligence of modern-day cocktail historians.

| CHAMPAGNE COCKTAIL |

Sparkling cocktails don't get more classic or elegant than this. If top-shelf Champagne fits your budget, this is the cocktail to show it off, but the touch of sugar and bitters gives a boost to less expensive bubbly, too.

1 cube raw sugar, or ½ teaspoon loose raw sugar

2 or 3 dashes of Angostura bitters

5 ounces Champagne brut or sparkling wine brut, chilled
(alternative: cava brut)

Lemon twist for garnish

Drop the sugar cube into a chilled 6-ounce flute. Wet the sugar with the bitters. Top slowly with the chilled Champagne. Stir gently. Garnish with a short strip of lemon peel, first twisting it over the glass to release the flavorful oils into the drink.

SERVES 1

For more citrus spice, substitute orange bitters for
the Angostura. Or try a mix: 2 dashes of Angostura and a dash of
orange bitters. Garnish with an orange twist instead of lemon.

SPIRITED CHAMPAGNE COCKTAIL:
For more warmth and depth of flavor, pour ½ ounce Cognac
over the bitters-soaked sugar cube before adding the Champagne.
Cocktail-swilling, world-traveling writer Charles Baker endorsed
this method in his 1939 *Gentleman's Companion*, which was
later republished as *Jigger, Beaker, & Glass*. A touch of Cognac
could hint at the flavor of nineteenth-century Champagnes,
which are said to have been sweeter and stronger than today's
bubbly. Alternatively, add ½ ounce of bourbon for a
Champagne Cocktail Americana, or ½ ounce of Calvados or
apple brandy for a Champagne Normande.

| FRENCH 75 |

A fixture in the 1920s and '30s at the Savoy in London and the Stork Club in New York, it's no coincidence that this virile cocktail is named for a French war gun. As barman Harry Craddock noted in *The Savoy Cocktail Book* in 1930, this drink "hits with remarkable precision."

1½ ounces gin

1½ ounces simple syrup (page 94)

¾ ounce freshly squeezed lemon juice

5 ounces Champagne brut or sparkling wine brut, chilled
(alternatives: cava brut, Sekt brut, Prosecco extra dry or brut)

Lemon twist for garnish

In a 10-ounce highball, combine the gin, simple syrup, and lemon juice and stir gently. Fill the glass halfway with cracked ice (see page 93). Top with the bubbly. Garnish with a short strip of lemon twist, first twisting it over the glass to release the flavorful oils into the drink.

SERVES 1

| BELLINI |

This peach of a drink was christened in 1948 at Harry's Bar in Venice, Italy. Giuseppe Cipriani had a soft spot for the region's white peaches and, determined to use them behind the bar, paired them with Prosecco, enhancing the wine's peach notes and unwittingly making cocktail history.

PEACH PURÉE

2 ripe white peaches
(yellow work, too, if you don't mind upsetting Giuseppe in his grave)
¼ ounce simple syrup (page 94), or more to taste
¼ ounce freshly squeezed lemon juice

16 ounces Prosecco, chilled
(alternatives: Asti, Moscato d'Asti, Sekt extra dry, sparkling ice wine)
8 dashes of peach bitters (optional)
4 thin slices peach for garnish (optional)
4 fresh basil leaves for garnish (optional)

To make the peach purée, wash and dry the peaches. Have ready a bowl of ice water. Cut an X in the skin on the bottom of each peach. Submerge in a pot of simmering water for 45 seconds to loosen the peels. Using a slotted spoon, transfer the peaches to the ice water for a few moments to stop the cooking process. Carefully pull the skin off the fruit. Cut the fruit into chunks, discarding the pits. Purée the chunks in a blender

cont'd

with the simple syrup and lemon juice, adding more syrup to taste if the peaches are not fully ripe or if you plan to use a very dry Prosecco. (Avoid over-sweetening—a natural peach flavor is ideal.) This should yield about 10 ounces of purée. Refrigerate until well chilled, at least 45 minutes.

In a shaker or pitcher, combine 8 ounces of the chilled peach purée with the chilled Prosecco (reserve any remaining purée for another use). Shake or stir well. Pour mixture into 4 chilled 6-ounce sparkling-wine glasses. For more peachy zing, dash each glass with peach bitters. For extra flair, garnish with a thin slice of peach and a basil leaf.

SERVES 4

Note: When peaches are in season, fresh purée is a must for a true Bellini. Other times, store-bought frozen purée or bottled nectar works fine; substitute 8 ounces for the fresh purée in the recipe.

SAME DRINK, DIFFERENT FRUIT:
Traditional variations replace the
peach with strawberry purée or grape juice.
Pear and apricot purées also work well.

JOIE DE PÊCHE:
At Boston's Eastern Standard
Kitchen & Drinks, mixologist Jackson Cannon
muddles half a fresh peach with 2 ounces
Lillet and ¼ ounce freshly squeezed
lemon juice. He shakes the concoction with
ice, strains it into a cocktail glass,
and tops with 2 ounces of cava.

| MIMOSA |

There's disagreement as to whether the Mimosa was invented at the Ritz Paris in 1925 or four years earlier at Buck's Club in London, where it's called the Buck's Fizz. Either way, ripe sweet oranges make this brunch staple sing.

2 to 2½ ounces freshly squeezed orange juice, such as Valencia, navel, mandarin, or blood orange

3½ to 4 ounces Champagne brut or sparkling wine brut, chilled (alternatives: cava brut, Sekt brut)

Pour the orange juice into a chilled 6-ounce flute. Top slowly with the chilled bubbly. Stir gently.

SERVES 1

Note: Fresh-pressed orange juice is always best, but if that requires more energy than you can muster before brunch, look for the freshest store-bought juice you can find.

| KIR ROYALE |

Black currant liqueur and white wine are a
classic match once favored by the French priest
and politician Félix Kir. Bubbly lends
a celebratory flair to Kir's cocktail.

1 ounce crème de cassis

**4 ½ ounces Champagne brut or sparkling wine brut, chilled
(alternatives: Prosecco extra dry or brut, cava brut, Sekt brut)**

Lemon twist for garnish

Pour the crème de cassis into a chilled 6-ounce sparkling-wine glass. Top
slowly with the chilled bubbly. Garnish with a short strip of lemon peel,
first twisting it over the glass to release the flavorful oils into the drink.

SERVES 1

cont'd

MUSICAL BERRIES:

Try substituting another fruit liqueur in place of the cassis.
For similar flavor, use another berry liqueur, like blackberry
(crème de mûre), raspberry (Chambord or crème de framboise)
or strawberry (crème de fraise). Or have fun with other fruits,
like peach, or a citrus liqueur that's on the sweet side.

MOCKTAIL:

Substitute black currant nectar or juice for the liqueur.
In place of sparkling wine, sub dry sparkling white grape juice
or soda, such as Vignette Wine Country Soda Chardonnay
or Seattle-made Dry Soda. If you choose an alcohol-free sparkler
that's on the sweet side, use less of it, topping the glass
with sparkling water.

| CHAMPAGNE VELVET |

Don't knock it till you try it. In 1939, Charles Baker said the Manila Polo Club's version was so good as to "save life, nourish, encourage, and induce sleep in insomniacs." The classic recipe calls for very dry Champagne, but soft, lightly sweet Asti is an easy-drinking alternative.

1 part stout, chilled

1 part Champagne brut or sparkling wine brut, chilled
(alternative: Asti)

Combine all the ingredients in a chilled goblet or saucer and stir gently.

SERVES 1

| CORPSE REVIVER NO. 2 |

"Corpse revivers"—morning-after tonics designed to snap the bleary-eyed back to attention—have been around in some form or another since the dawn of the cocktail. This version is based on a Ritz Paris classic.

½ ounce freshly squeezed lemon juice

1½ ounces absinthe, Pernod, or other pastis, chilled

2 ounces Champagne brut or sparkling wine brut, chilled
(alternatives: cava brut, Prosecco brut)

2 real maraschino cherries for garnish (optional)

2 sprigs fresh thyme for garnish (optional)

In a shaker, combine the lemon juice, absinthe, and Champagne and shake vigorously with ice. Strain into 2 chilled 2-ounce cordial glasses. If you like, place a maraschino cherry and a thyme sprig in each glass to soften and round the anise-heavy tipple. Drink it while it's cold.

SERVES 2

| STRATOSPHERE |

The sweet Muscat and acidic berry notes
of Italy's Moscato d'Asti are lovely with the
delicate, floral violet liqueur in this adaptation
of a recipe from Lucius Beebe's 1946 classic,
The Stork Club Bar Book. The original recipe
called for Champagne.

2 whole cloves

³/₄ ounce crème de violette

**5 ounces Moscato d'Asti, chilled
(alternatives: Asti, Prosecco extra dry, Champagne extra dry)**

Lemon twist for garnish

Place the cloves in a chilled 6-ounce sparkling-wine glass. Add the crème
de violette. Top slowly with the chilled bubbly. Stir gently. Garnish with
short strip of lemon peel, first twisting it over the glass to release the
flavorful oils into the drink.

SERVES 1

| SEELBACH COCKTAIL |

Make this drink for your bourbon-obsessed friend who thinks he doesn't like bubbly cocktails. The pre-Prohibition specialty of the Seelbach Hotel in Louisville, Kentucky, it tastes like a fizzy Old-Fashioned.

1 ounce bourbon

$^1/_2$ ounce Cointreau

7 dashes of Angostura bitters

7 dashes of Peychaud's bitters

4$^1/_2$ ounces Champagne brut or sparkling wine brut, chilled
(alternatives: cava brut, Sekt brut)

Real maraschino cherry for garnish

Orange twist for garnish

In a shaker, combine all but the Champagne and garnishes and shake vigorously with ice. Strain into a chilled 6-ounce sparkling-wine glass. Top slowly with the chilled Champagne. Stir gently. Garnish with a cherry and short strip of orange peel, first twisting it over the glass to release the flavorful oils into the drink.

SERVES 1

| TWO JULEPS |

These nineteenth-century juleps may not be as well-known as their sibling, the mint julep, but they're equally refreshing.

CHAMPAGNE JULEP

½ ounce simple syrup (page 94)

2 sprigs fresh mint

Dash of apple or pear brandy

5 ounces Champagne brut or sparkling wine brut, chilled (alternative: cava brut)

Fresh berries or thin slices of apple or pear for garnish

In a 10-ounce highball glass, muddle the simple syrup and mint. Dash with the brandy. Fill the glass one-third full with cracked ice (see page 93). Top slowly with the Champagne. Stir gently. Garnish with fresh berries.

SERVES 1

cont'd

PINEAPPLE JULEP

4 small cubes fresh pineapple

$3/4$ ounce freshly squeezed orange juice

2 teaspoons raspberry preserves

$3/4$ ounce maraschino liqueur

$3/4$ ounce gin

$4 1/2$ ounces Sekt, chilled

(alternatives: cava extra dry, Champagne extra dry, sparkling wine extra dry)

2 spears fresh pineapple for garnish

Orange twist for garnish

Fresh berries for garnish (optional)

In a shaker, muddle the pineapple cubes and orange juice. Add the raspberry preserves, maraschino liqueur, and gin. Shake with ice and strain into a 10-ounce highball glass. Fill glass one-third full with crushed ice (see Note and page 93). Top slowly with Sekt. Stir gently. Garnish with pineapple spears and a short strip of orange peel, first twisting it over the glass to release the flavorful oils into the drink. Add fresh berries, if using.

SERVES 1

Note: You can use a powerful blender to make crushed ice. My Blendtec has an ice-crushing feature that chips large cubes down to tiny chips or even a snowlike consistency in a matter of seconds, keeping the ice dry and not slushy. Check your blender manual to see if it can handle ice.

| CHAMPAGNE COBBLER |

An exceedingly refreshing drink, this Cobbler looks like a garden party in a glass and begs for back-porch summer sipping—but don't overlook the nineteenth-century dazzler for more formal occasions. In pre-Prohibition St. Louis, barman Tom Bullock served his with a straw.

One 5-inch strip lemon peel

One 5-inch strip orange peel

¼ ounce simple syrup (page 94)

2 thin slices cucumber

2 sprigs fresh mint

2 fresh berries (optional)

6 ounces Champagne brut or sparkling wine brut
(alternatives: cava brut, Prosecco extra dry or brut, Sekt brut)

Real maraschino cherry for garnish

In a 10-ounce highball glass, muddle the citrus peels with the simple syrup. Add the cucumber, mint, and the berries, if using. Fill the glass halfway with crushed ice (see page 93). Top slowly with the bubbly, stirring gently. Garnish with a cherry.

SERVES 1

| CRIMEAN CUP À LA MARMORA |

Everyone who tries this punch loves it. Another nineteenth-century cocktail immortalized by Jerry Thomas in his Civil War–era bartending manual, *How to Mix Drinks, or the Bon Vivant's Companion*, this is one recipe you might choose to double or triple, because it goes fast.

¾ medium lemon, cut into thin slices

1 ounce simple syrup (page 94)

3 ounces Cognac

1¼ ounces aged rum

1¼ ounces maraschino liqueur

3 ounces orgeat syrup

6 ounces sparkling water, chilled

8 ounces Champagne brut or sparkling wine brut, chilled
(alternatives: cava brut, Prosecco extra dry or brut, Sekt brut)

Real maraschino cherries for garnish

In a pitcher, muddle the lemon and simple syrup. Add the Cognac, rum, maraschino liqueur, and orgeat syrup, stirring to combine. Top slowly with the chilled sparkling water and Champagne. Pour into punch glasses over a few pieces of ice. Garnish each with a cherry.

SERVES 5

| BOMBAY PUNCH |

When Prohibition wiped out U.S. cocktail culture, American barman Harry Craddock didn't cry into his root beer—he left for London's Savoy Hotel, where he mixed this deceptively strong punch for Londoners, American expats, and other thirsty travelers.

6 thin slices lemon

6 thin slices orange

$1/4$ cup raw sugar

4 ounces brandy

4 ounces sherry

$1/2$ ounce maraschino liqueur

$1/2$ ounce orange curaçao

8 ounces sparkling water, chilled

16 ounces Champagne brut or sparkling wine brut, chilled
(alternatives: cava brut, Prosecco extra dry or brut, Sekt brut)

Fresh berries or pineapple for garnish

Fresh basil leaves for garnish (optional)

cont'd

In a pitcher or punch bowl, toss the citrus slices with the sugar and let sit for 5 minutes to macerate. Add the brandy, sherry, maraschino liqueur, and orange curaçao, stirring to combine. Top slowly with the sparkling water and Champagne. Garnish with berries or pineapple and basil leaves, if using. Pour or ladle into punch glasses over a few pieces of ice.

SERVES 6

Note: Keep your punch bowl cool by snuggling it into a larger ice-filled holder, or float a large, slow-melting brick of ice in the bowl. (Fill a cake pan with ice and freeze it overnight to make an appropriately sized iceberg.)

CHAPTER 3

New Classics

Sparkling wine still isn't as popular in the States as in Europe, but it has seen a boost on bar menus and wine lists lately. Prosecco in particular has been discovered as a versatile mixer, thanks to its soft bubbles and smooth body. Most of the sparkling cocktails gracing drink menus these days seem to be inspired by Prosecco-based Italian concoctions, but here, classic-inspired Champagne cocktails are represented, too. Most of the fourteen new classics in this chapter use garden-fresh fruit, juices, and herbs, and some call for new-fangled bubblies like sparkling sake and fizzy Australian Shiraz. Here's to progress—and to keeping it in check.

| OLD CUBAN |

Audrey Saunders, founder of Manhattan's cocktail hub, the Pegu Club, created this cocktail because she loves Mojitos but wanted something more elegant that she could serve year-round. "This drink is just as welcome on New Year's Eve as it would be on July 4th—a Mojito in a little black cocktail dress," she says.

¾ ounce freshly squeezed lime juice

1 ounce simple syrup (page 94)

6 fresh mint leaves

1½ ounces aged rum

2 dashes of Angostura bitters

2 ounces Champagne brut or sparkling wine brut, chilled
(alternatives: cava brut, Prosecco brut)

Fresh vanilla bean rolled in fine sugar

In a shaker, muddle the lime juice, simple syrup, and mint. Add the rum and bitters and shake vigorously with ice. Strain into a chilled 6-ounce sparkling-wine glass. Top slowly with the chilled bubbly. Garnish with a vanilla bean.

SERVES 1

| FOUR Bs |

Here's another drink to school whiskey lovers who think they don't like Champagne cocktails. Like a fizzy Manhattan with a touch of Bénédictine's herbs and honey, this recipe is easy to remember thanks to the name: bourbon, Bénedictine, bitters, and bubbly—the Four Bs.

³/₄ ounce bourbon

¹/₄ ounce Bénédictine

Dash of bitters

**3 ounces Champagne brut or sparkling wine brut, chilled
(alternative: cava brut, Prosecco extra dry or brut)**

Real maraschino cherry for garnish

In a shaker, combine the bourbon, Bénédictine, and bitters and shake vigorously with ice. Strain into a chilled 6-ounce sparkling-wine glass. Top slowly with the chilled bubbly. Garnish with a cherry.

SERVES 1

| SOUTH SIDE FIZZ |

This bubbly interpretation of the South Side cocktail is a favorite at the Zig Zag Café in Seattle. It would make a mighty fine cooler in an ice-filled tall glass, but at Zig Zag they keep it smart and subtle, served up, no garnish.

1 slice orange

1 slice lemon

4 large fresh mint leaves

¼ ounce gin

⅛ ounce Cointreau

4 ounces Champagne brut or sparkling wine brut, chilled
(alternatives: cava brut, Prosecco extra dry or brut)

In a shaker, muddle the citrus slices, mint, gin, and Cointreau. Shake vigorously with ice. Strain into a chilled 6-ounce sparkling-wine glass and top slowly with the chilled bubbly.

SERVES 1

| ORANGE YOU GLAD |

I created this drink to celebrate the drink magazine *Imbibe*'s first birthday. Honey, basil, and sweet orange mingle amorously with the wine-based herbal aperitif Lillet and dry, velvety Prosecco. If the Mimosa is a brunch drink, this is its black-tie cousin.

1 slice fresh, ripe orange

½ ounce honey syrup (equal parts honey and hot water, stirred to combine)

2 dashes of orange bitters

1 ounce Lillet

1 or 2 small leaves fresh basil

4 ounces Prosecco extra dry, chilled
(alternatives: cava extra dry, Asti, Champagne extra dry, sparkling wine extra dry)

Small basil leaf for garnish

Orange twist for garnish

In a shaker, muddle the orange slice, honey syrup, and bitters. Add the Lillet and stir. Add the basil, fill the shaker half-full with ice cubes, and shake vigorously. Strain into a chilled 6-ounce flute and top slowly with the chilled bubbly. Garnish with a basil leaf and a short strip of orange peel, first twisting it over the glass to release the flavorful oils into the drink.

SERVES 1

| MARASCA FIZZ |

Geoffrey Zakarian is serious about bubbly.
There's a Champagne bar in the dining room
of his New York City restaurant, Country.
This cocktail is the cherry on top.

Loose raw sugar for the rim of the glass

4 real maraschino cherries with syrup

2 cubes raw sugar

3 dashes of Angostura bitters

1 ounce kirschwasser or other cherry brandy

4 ounces Champagne brut or sparkling wine brut, chilled
(alternatives: cava brut, Sekt brut, Prosecco extra dry or brut)

Place a little loose sugar on a small plate. Wipe 1 cherry along the rim
of a chilled 6-ounce flute, then turn the glass over and dip the rim in the
sugar. Put the sugar cubes in the glass and add the bitters, kirshwasser,
and 3 remaining cherries, each with a dash of the syrup they're packed in.
Top slowly with the chilled bubbly and stir gently.

SERVES 1

| CANADIAN BEAUTY |

Crisp, sweet, ice wines are gorgeous with very dry sparkling wines. This recipe was inspired by a 1950s cocktail, the American Beauty, which called simply for muscatel—a sweet still wine—and Champagne.

1 ounce ice wine, chilled

4 ounces Champagne brut or sparkling wine brut, chilled (alternative: cava brut)

1 sprig fresh basil

2 fresh gooseberries

In a shaker, combine all the ingredients with a handful of ice cubes. Shake vigorously, then pour the contents into a 10-ounce highball glass. Add additional ice cubes to fill the glass.

SERVES 1

| DINING CAR |

This recipe makes a great brunch alternative to the Mimosa, but don't confine it to daytime—bright, tart, pink grapefruit juice can be like liquid sunshine on an otherwise dreary winter evening. For a Rio fizz, use Texas-grown grapefruit and a Texas-made sparkling wine.

1½ ounces freshly squeezed pink grapefruit juice, chilled

Splash of Cointreau

1 or 2 splashes of simple syrup (page 94)

4 ounces Prosecco extra dry, chilled
(alternatives: Champagne extra dry, sparkling wine extra dry, cava extra dry, Asti)

Grapefruit twist for garnish

Pour the grapefruit juice into a chilled 6-ounce sparkling-wine glass. Stir in the Cointreau and simple syrup to taste. Top slowly with the chilled bubbly, stirring gently. Garnish with a short strip of grapefruit peel, first twisting it over the glass to release the flavorful oils into the drink.

SERVES 1

| FRAGOLINO |

Umberto Gibin, co-owner of Perbacco in San Francisco, created this fun, refreshing cocktail with summer in mind. Sweet, ripe strawberries make it irresistible.

1 ounce fresh strawberry purée, chilled

¾ ounce Aperol (or Campari, in a pinch)

4 ounces Prosecco extra dry or brut, chilled (alternative: Asti)

1 fresh, ripe strawberry, for garnish

In a chilled 6-ounce sparkling-wine glass, gently stir together the strawberry purée and Aperol. Top slowly with the chilled Prosecco and stir gently. Garnish with the strawberry.

SERVES 1

BERRY SWEET:

If the strawberry purée isn't sweet enough, add a splash of simple syrup (page 94) and freshly squeezed lemon juice to taste.

| MELAGRANA |

This recipe from A Voce in New York City celebrates the enchantingly sweet-tart combination of limoncello, pomegranate juice, and bubbly. Portland's Paragon uses a Northwest sparkling wine brut instead of Prosecco, and calls it a Fever—an appropriate name for the rosy, palate-pleasing drink.

1 ounce limoncello

1 ounce pomegranate juice

3 ½ ounces Prosecco brut, chilled
(alternatives: Champagne brut or sparkling wine brut)

Lemon twist for garnish

In a shaker, combine the limoncello and pomegranate juice and shake vigorously with ice. Strain into a chilled 6-ounce sparkling-wine glass. Top slowly with the chilled Prosecco and stir gently. Garnish with a short strip of lemon peel, first twisting it over the glass to release the flavorful oils into the drink.

SERVES 1

| SPRITZ |

Choose your own adventure with this convertible recipe. Any Italian bitter or herbal liqueur will do. Drink it before dinner, as an aperitivo.

1½ ounces bitter or herbal liqueur such as Campari, Cynar, Aperol, or Strega

3 ounces Prosecco extra dry, chilled (alternative: Asti)

1½ ounces sparkling water, chilled

Orange or lemon wedge for garnish

Pour the liqueur into a chilled 6-ounce sparkling-wine glass. Top slowly with the chilled Prosecco and sparkling water, stirring gently. Garnish with a citrus wedge.

SERVES 1

FRENCH TWIST: If you're feeling more Paris than Milan, substitute a French herbal liqueur in place of the Italian bitter. Then add Champagne extra dry or another French sparkler instead of Prosecco and voilà—instant aperitif for predinner sipping. St. Germain, Farigoule, Elisir M.P. Roux, and Chartreuse all work well with bubbly and a lemon wedge, in the same proportions given in this recipe.

| VALENTINE |

This pretty pink cocktail, inspired by a love potion served at London's Savoy Hotel in the 1920s, has a dainty floral aroma and flavor. The raspberry bits that float on the surface look like a dozen tiny rose petals. Perfect for Valentine's Day, weddings, showers, and anniversaries.

2 fresh, ripe raspberries

¾ ounce maraschino liqueur

¾ ounce crème de violette

4 ounces Prosecco extra dry, chilled (alternatives: Moscato d'Asti, Asti)

Lemon twist for garnish

In a shaker, muddle the raspberries, maraschino liqueur, and crème de violette, then shake vigorously with ice. Strain into a chilled 6-ounce sparkling-wine glass. Top slowly with the chilled bubbly, stirring gently. Garnish with a short strip of lemon peel, first twisting it over the glass to release the flavorful oils into the drink.

SERVES 1

HOW SWEET IS LOVE:
Prosecco balances the sweet cherry liqueur and crème de violette,
but if you're willing to kick up the floral bouquet a notch, try using
Moscato d'Asti—it's sweet, but the rich, gorgeous flavor is a good
match, and fresh raspberries and lemon peel keep the drink bright.

| STRAWBERRY-PROSECCO LEMONADE |

It's hard to argue with lemonade, especially if it involves Prosecco, fresh strawberries, and the irresistible Bonny Doon framboise. It's equally delicious with basil or mint, so take your pick.

2 fresh, ripe strawberries

1 large sprig fresh basil or mint

¾ ounce freshly squeezed lemon juice

¼ ounce simple syrup (page 94)

¾ ounce Bonny Doon framboise

3 ounces Prosecco extra dry or brut, chilled
(alternatives: cava brut, Champagne brut, sparkling wine brut)

Splash of sparkling water

In a 10-ounce highball glass, muddle the strawberries, basil, lemon juice, and simple syrup. Fill the glass three-quarters full with ice. Add the framboise. Top slowly with the Prosecco and sparkling water, stirring gently.

SERVES 1

| ARCHBISHOP DOWN UNDER |

This nineteenth-century sangria is made new when sparkling Australian Shiraz stands in for the traditional port. The bold, oaky, berry-noted bubbly is complemented by dark, sweet aged rum and bright lime.

2 small limes, cut into thin slices

2 ounces freshly squeezed lime juice

6 lychees, canned, peeled

10 to 12 fresh, ripe berries
(or unsweetened frozen berries, thawed, in a pinch)

1 ounce simple syrup (page 94)

2 ounces aged rum

8 ounces sparkling Australian Shiraz, chilled

8 ounces sparkling water, chilled

Put the lime slices in a pitcher and add the lime juice (squeezed from additional limes), lychees, berries, simple syrup, and rum. Stir to combine. Let sit for 5 minutes to macerate, then stir gently but well. Cover the pitcher and refrigerate for 30 minutes to 1 hour. Top slowly with the sparkling wine and water, stirring gently. Pour into punch glasses over a few pieces of ice.

SERVES 5

| SPARKLING SAKE, SUSPENDED MELON |

Aside from the novelty of an all-white sangria punctuated by floating balls of melon, which is reason enough to mix up a batch, this drink tastes fantastic. The tart, fruity, gently effervescent sake complements all kinds of melon available throughout the year.

8 to 10 small balls ripe melon

6 lychees, canned, peeled

2 ounces freshly squeezed lemon juice

1 ounce agave nectar

4 ounces light rum

12 ounces sparkling sake, chilled

8 ounces sparkling water, chilled

In a pitcher or bowl, combine the melon balls, lychees, lemon juice, agave nectar, and rum. Stir to combine. Let sit for 5 minutes to macerate, then stir again. Top slowly with the sparkling sake and water, stirring gently. Pour or ladle into punch glasses over a few pieces of ice.

SERVES 5

CHAPTER 4

Mocktails

Designated drivers, pregnant women, kids, and guests who just don't feel like getting tipsy shouldn't be left out when the bubbly starts to flow. Just because they're abstaining doesn't mean they actually enjoy drinking soda water with lime all night. These four mocktails are fresh and fizzy (without the dizzy). And for goodness' sake, serve them in real glasses, not plastic cups.

Tip: When in doubt: make it a Mimosa. Mix the freshest orange or tangerine juice you can get with a not-too-sweet sparkling soda or juice and serve it in an attractive glass. Instant mocktail.

| FAUXLLINI |

If you seek the velvety, peachy goodness of a Bellini without the buzz, try one of these two formulas. The first calls for Dry Soda Rhubarb, one of the brilliantly whispery flavors from the Seattle-based soda maker Dry Soda. The second pairs fresh basil with a grape-based sparkler.

RHUBARB FAUXLLINI

12 ounces peach purée or nectar, chilled

12 ounces Dry Soda Rhubarb, chilled

In a pitcher, combine the chilled peach purée and soda, stirring well. Pour into glasses, straight or over ice.

SERVES 4

cont'd

| SPARKLING PEAR FLOAT |

You're never too old for a root beer float, but if you're looking for something fruity, this sparkling float might suit you. It tastes like a spicy Creamsicle, with a side of fizzy pear. For the best results, use a marmalade that's as bitter as it is sweet, with lots of orange peel.

2 to 3 medium scoops vanilla ice cream

Fresh berries or real maraschino cherries

½ ounce Clove Syrup (recipe on page 70)

2 teaspoons orange marmalade

Sparkling pear juice or cider, chilled

Spoon the ice cream into a saucer or a highball. Add the desired amount of fresh berries. In a separate cup or small bowl, mix together the Clove Syrup and orange marmalade, stirring well. Drizzle the orange-clove mixture over the ice cream and fruit. Top with the chilled sparkling pear juice. Serve with a spoon.

SERVES 1

cont'd

CLOVE SYRUP

1 cup raw sugar

1 cup water

⅓ cup whole cloves

In a small saucepan over medium heat, combine all the ingredients and bring close to a boil, stirring constantly, then reduce heat to low and simmer for 20 minutes, stirring occasionally. Let cool at room temperature. Strain into a clean bottle, cover, and refrigerate until ready to use. The syrup will keep for up to 2 weeks in the refrigerator.

MAKES 1 CUP

| ALMOND-BERRY FIZZ |

The warm almond flavor of orgeat syrup anchors the tart lemon and fresh raspberries in this palate-tingler. Serve it in a sparkling-wine glass, for a mocktail that fits in with a roomful of cocktails.

4 large fresh raspberries, or 1 teaspoon low-sugar raspberry preserves

1 tablespoon orgeat syrup

3/4 ounce freshly squeezed lemon juice

1 tablespoon honey

2 ounces white wine—based soda, such as Vignette Wine Country Soda Chardonnay, or a not-too-sweet sparkling white grape juice, chilled

2 ounces sparkling water, chilled

In a shaker, combine the raspberries, orgeat syrup, lemon juice, and honey and shake vigorously with ice. (Omit the honey if you're substituting preserves for the raspberries.) Strain into a chilled sparkling-wine glass. Add the chilled sparkling soda or juice. Top with the chilled sparkling water. Stir gently.

SERVES 1

CHAPTER 5

Bubbly Bites

You may be surprised to learn that the
cherry in your Seelbach Cocktail isn't an adequate
food source. No, humans cannot live on bubbly
cocktails alone. You're going to need to nibble on
something. The good news is that sparkling wine
can go from glass to plate. Each of the eight
small bites in this chapter not only pairs well with
bubbly but also includes the fizzy stuff as a vital
ingredient. Plus, all the recipes are easy to make,
so there's no need to dim a festive occasion with
too much fussing in the kitchen.

LIGHT AND CRISPY TEMPURA ONION RINGS
WITH SPICY SPARKLING KETCHUP

Sparkling sake tempura makes these rings light and a little crispy. It also adds plate appeal—the thinly sliced red onions peek through the fried tempura for an effect that's almost too pretty to eat. Almost. The Spicy Sparkling Ketchup is a cinch—sweet and spicy, with ninja-like berry notes.

SPICY SPARKLING KETCHUP

1 red bell pepper, freshly roasted, seeded, and coarsely chopped

2 1/4 cups sweet cherry tomatoes, halved

2 cups coarsely chopped red onion

2 or 3 cloves garlic, diced

1 teaspoon sea salt

1 teaspoon black peppercorns

1/4 teaspoon coriander seeds

1/4 teaspoon cumin seeds

1/4 teaspoon grated fresh horseradish root or prepared horseradish
(not the creamy kind)

2 teaspoons raw sugar

3 tablespoons Champagne vinegar

2 tablespoons sparkling red wine such as Australian Shiraz

cont'd

2 large eggs

1⅓ cups sparkling sake, well chilled

1½ cups pastry flour

1 teaspoon sea salt

2 medium red or sweet onions

Light-flavored oil such as sunflower for frying

Table salt or finely ground sea salt for sprinkling

To make the ketchup: In a blender or food processor, combine all the ingredients and purée to an even consistency. You should have about 4 cups of ketchup. Cover and set aside or refrigerate while you prepare the tempura.

To make the tempura: Beat the eggs in a large bowl. Whisk in the sparkling sake. In a smaller bowl, combine the flour and salt. Whisk the flour-salt mixture into the egg mixture ½ cup at a time, by hand or with an electric mixer, until smooth. You should have 4 to 5 cups of batter. Cover and refrigerate while you prepare the onions.

Slice the onions into medium-thin rings (about ¼ inch thick). In a deep skillet, heat about 2 inches of frying oil over medium heat for about 4 minutes, to 375°F on a deep-frying thermometer or until a test drop of tempura batter puffs up instantly and holds its shape. Dip the onion rings into the batter to coat, one at a time, and immediately transfer to the skillet, always being careful around the hot oil. Using a large slotted spoon, turn the onion rings to fry both sides to a lightly golden color, about 1 minute total. Transfer the cooked onion rings to a paper towel–lined plate for a few seconds to blot the excess oil. Salt to taste. Serve with the Spicy Sparkling Ketchup.

SERVES 6

CHAMPAGNE WILD MUSHROOMS
ON MINI CRÊPES

As if rich, creamy sautéed mushrooms aren't dreamy enough, Champagne takes them up a notch, lending a soft, elegant bite. Try not to eat them all out of the pan before you get them onto the adorable, herb-kissed crêpes.

MINI CRÊPE BATTER

3 tablespoons unsalted butter

2 eggs

¼ cup cold milk

2 teaspoons finely chopped fresh rosemary

½ cup pastry flour

¼ teaspoon sea salt

cont'd

CHAMPAGNE WILD MUSHROOMS

3 tablespoons unsalted butter

6 cups wild mushrooms, stemmed and coarsely chopped

¼ cup minced shallots

2 tablespoons finely chopped fresh thyme

½ cup heavy cream

½ cup Champagne brut or sparkling wine brut

Sea salt to taste

Freshly ground black pepper to taste

To make the crêpe batter: Melt 1 tablespoon of the butter, then let cool to room temperature. Place a large glass bowl in the freezer for a few minutes to chill. Add the eggs to the chilled bowl and beat to blend. Whisk in the melted and cooled butter, cold milk, and rosemary. In a smaller bowl, combine the flour and salt. Whisk the dry mixture into the egg mixture until smooth. Cover and refrigerate while you sauté the mushrooms.

To make the mushrooms: In a large sauté pan, melt the butter over medium-high heat. Add the mushrooms and sauté for about 3 minutes until partially cooked. Push the mushrooms to the side and add the shallots, sautéing for about 1 minute, stirring constantly. Add the thyme and sauté for another minute, stirring constantly. Mix the mushrooms in with shallots and thyme and sauté for another 3 minutes, until cooked through. Reduce heat to a simmer and add the cream and Champagne. Salt and pepper to taste. While the sauce reduces and thickens, prepare the crêpes.

In a buttered, medium-hot skillet, pour 1 tablespoon crêpe batter to make a crêpe about 3 inches in diameter, lightly browning each side. Repeat, holding the finished crêpes in a warm oven. To serve, spoon the mushroom sauce over the mini crêpes.

SERVES 6

GARLIC-APPLE FOLD-OVERS
WITH BUBBLY CHEESE FILLING

Ever since I sampled a crisp, sweet-tart apple that had been accidentally cozying up to a fresh garlic bulb in my fruit bowl, I've been hooked on the combo. I like my pastries more savory than sweet, and these are just right. They go fast, so save one for yourself.

$\frac{1}{2}$ cup raw sugar

$2\frac{1}{2}$ tablespoons ground cinnamon

6 cloves garlic, minced

1 firm, sweet-tart apple, peeled, cored, and cut into $\frac{1}{8}$-inch-thick slices

2 frozen puff pastry sheets, thawed and cut into eight 4-inch squares

2 large eggs

3 tablespoons cold water

BUBBLY CHEESE FILLING

8 ounces mascarpone

1 tablespoon butter, softened

1 tablespoon cava brut or sparkling wine brut

Generous pinch of salt

cont'd

Preheat the oven to 400°F. In a medium bowl, stir together the sugar, cinnamon, and garlic. Add 16 to 24 apple slices to the sugar mixture (this is all the apple you'll need to make 8 fold-overs), tossing well and using your hands to gently rub the mixture into the slices. Let the apple slices sit in the sugar mixture while you prepare the other ingredients. Place the puff pastry squares on 2 ungreased baking sheets. In a bowl, beat together the eggs and water. Brush a thin layer of the egg mixture onto the top of each pastry square.

To make the filling: In a bowl, using an electric mixer, beat the mascarpone, butter, cava, and salt together with one-quarter of the remaining egg mixture until smooth, thick, and shiny.

Imagine an invisible line drawn diagonally from the upper left corner to the lower right corner of each pastry square, where you will fold the filled square in half. In the middle of the lower left triangle of each square, spoon 1½ teaspoons of the cheese mixture. Place 1 to 3 apple slices on top of the cheese (depending on the size of the slices), cutting long slices to fit. Do not overfill the pastry. Fold the square in half diagonally to cover the filling, sealing the edges by folding the sides of the bottom layer slightly over the sides of the top layer and pressing gently. Brush the remaining egg mixture over the tops and sides of each fold-over. Cut a small line in the top of each fold-over, so air can release during baking. Bake for 12 to 16 minutes, or until golden brown. Let cool for at least 5 minutes before serving.

SERVES 8

BEET AND SWEET POTATO TACOS
WITH CARROT SALSA AND CAVA CILANTRO SAUCE

Purple, gold, orange, and green, these tacos are a feast for the eyes. The wow factor starts before the first bite, and, conveniently, they taste as good as they look. Plus, the easy Carrot Salsa is a great way to sneak veggies into your party snacks.

CAVA CILANTRO SAUCE

1 cup sour cream

$\frac{1}{3}$ cup cava brut or sparkling wine brut

2 cups coarsely chopped fresh cilantro

2 tablespoons freshly squeezed lime juice

1 generous pinch sea salt

1 generous pinch ground cumin

CARROT SALSA

1 cup coarsely chopped carrots

$\frac{1}{3}$ cup coarsely chopped red onion

$\frac{1}{4}$ cup diced ripe tomato

2 cloves garlic, diced

$\frac{1}{4}$ to $\frac{1}{2}$ small habanero chile, coarsely chopped (optional)

1 tablespoon freshly squeezed lime juice

Pinch of raw sugar

$\frac{1}{4}$ teaspoon sea salt

cont'd

10 small tortillas

3 cups 1/2-inch-diced cooked beets

3 cups 1/2-inch-diced cooked sweet potatoes

1 1/2 cups shredded green cabbage

Flaxseeds (optional)

Lime wedges for serving

To make the Cava Cilantro Sauce: In a blender or food processor, purée the ingredients until the color reaches an even, bright green. Cover and refrigerate while you prepare the Carrot Salsa. To make the salsa, loosely purée all the ingredients in a blender or food processor, leaving the salsa slightly chunky. For a milder salsa, remove the spicy seeds and use only the flesh of the chile.

To assemble the tacos: Steam or pan-warm the tortillas. (You can also wrap the tortillas in damp paper towels and microwave them briefly.) Place about 1/4 cup of beets and an equal amount of sweet potatoes in the middle of each tortilla. Top with the cabbage, Carrot Salsa, and Cava Cilantro Sauce. Optionally, sprinkle flaxseeds on top for extra crunch and a rich, nutty flavor. Serve with lime wedges.

SERVES 10

BEET AND AVOCADO SALAD
WITH SPARKLING LIME VINAIGRETTE

This citrusy vinaigrette was inspired by a tequila-based dressing I had in Mexico. The lime, chili powder, agave nectar, and basil mirror the fresh, piquant tastes of Jalisco and complement the avocado and grapefruit that grow in the region. Beets bring it all home.

2 cups roasted red and gold beet wedges

2 cups avocado wedges

2 cups ruby red grapefruit wedges

¼ cup thinly sliced red onion

¼ cup crumbled feta

2 tablespoons finely chopped fresh basil

cont'd

SPARKLING LIME VINAIGRETTE
2 tablespoons freshly squeezed lime juice

2 tablespoons champagne vinegar

3 tablespoons sunflower oil

1½ tablespoons cava brut or sparkling wine brut

1 teaspoon agave nectar

1 tablespoon finely chopped fresh basil

¼ teaspoon chili powder

¼ teaspoon sea salt

¼ teaspoon black pepper

sea salt

freshly ground black pepper

Combine the beets, avocado, grapefruit, onion, feta, and basil in a bowl. Set aside. To make the vinaigrette, combine all the ingredients in a glass jar with a lid. Cover tightly and shake well. Pour 2 to 3 tablespoons of the vinaigrette onto the salad, tossing gently. Add more vinaigrette if needed. Arrange the salad on 4 plates. Add salt and pepper to taste.

SERVES 4

FIZZY MELON SOUP

This zesty, chilled soup is perfect in the summer, when it's too hot to turn on the stove. Any type of melon works, from easy-to-find supermarket varieties to farmers' market heirloom beauties. Sparkling sake adds its own rich melon notes and soft fizz.

6 cups cubed fresh, ripe melon

4 tablespoons finely chopped fresh mint

1 cup fresh, ripe raspberries

1 orange, peeled, pithed, and separated into segments

1 tablespoon freshly squeezed lime juice

2 tablespoons agave nectar

2 teaspoons peeled and grated fresh ginger

1/4 teaspoon sea salt

3/4 cup sparkling sake

Reserve 2 cups of the melon and 2 tablespoons of the mint for garnish. In a blender or food processor, combine all the remaining ingredients except the sake. Purée until consistently blended. Pour the sake into the purée, stirring gently but well. Refrigerate the soup for at least 2 hours. In the meantime, cut the reserved melon into 1/2-inch dice. When the soup is chilled, stir gently but well. Spoon into bowls and garnish with the reserved melon and mint.

SERVES 8

PUNCHY STRAWBERRY POMSICLES

The garish tunes of the neighborhood ice cream truck may not be the highlight of your summer afternoons anymore, but these grown-up Popsicles might be. They're tangy and sweet, with an irresistibly supple texture. No calliope tunes required—your friends will come running.

4 cups fresh, ripe strawberries, quartered

1½ cups pomegranate juice

½ cup Prosecco

2 tablespoons agave nectar

In a blender, juicer, or food processor, purée all the ingredients well. Pour into Popsicle molds and freeze for at least 8 hours.

Note: When strawberries aren't in season, frozen strawberries work fine. Reduce the amount of agave nectar if the frozen berries are already sweetened. Also reduce the amount of agave if you use a pomegranate juice that's sweetened with sugar or other fruits.

SERVES 10

EASY CHAMPAGNE CHOCOLATE TRUFFLES

These rich, creamy chocolate treats look and taste impressive, but they're about as easy as whipping up a batch of cookies. Pair them with the Champagne Cocktail (page 16) or the French 75 (page 18).

2 ounces unsweetened chocolate, broken into pieces

½ tablespoon heavy whipping cream

1 tablespoon butter, grated

2½ tablespoons confectioners' sugar, plus more to taste

2 drops orange oil

¼ teaspoon vanilla extract

1 tablespoon Champagne brut or sparkling wine brut

¼ cup unsweetened cocoa powder or unsweetened chocolate shavings

cont'd

In a double boiler or metal bowl set on top of a pot of simmering water, melt the chocolate pieces, cream, and butter over medium heat, stirring constantly. When melted, add powdered sugar, orange oil, vanilla, and Champagne, continuing to stir until smooth and thick. Remove from heat and let the chocolate mixture cool for 10 minutes. Cover and refrigerate for another 15 minutes, or until firm enough to roll into balls. Remove from the refrigerator and use your hands to roll the chocolate into 10 half-tablespoon balls. Roll the balls in the cocoa to cover, and place on a parchment paper–lined plate or baking sheet. Let soften at room temperature for at least 20 minutes before serving.

Note: For even faster, easier truffles without the round shape or the coating of cocoa, press the warm chocolate mixture into a silicone ice cube tray, or a plastic ice cube tray with its cups lined with parchment paper squares. Cover and refrigerate for about 30 minutes, or until firm. Warm at room temperature for at least 10 minutes before serving.

SERVES 10

| GLOSSARY |

Agave nectar, agave syrup A liquid sweetener made from the agave plant. Both forms are sweeter than honey and table sugar.

Angostura The most commonly used brand of bitters.

Aperitif, aperitivo A pre-meal drink designed to prep the digestive system for food.

Asti A somewhat sweet, fruity, moderately sparkling Italian wine made from Muscat grapes.

Bénédictine A longstanding French herbal liqueur with light honey and spice notes.

Bitters A very potent liquid spice used to add dimension to cocktails. Common brands include Angostura, Peychaud's, Fee Brothers, and Regan's. Fee Brothers makes a range of bitters, some flavored with orange, peach, lemon, or mint.

Brut Very dry.

Calvados French apple brandy made in the Calvados region.

Cava A Spanish sparkling wine similar to Champagne.

Champagne A fully sparkling wine made according to strict tradition in the Champagne region of France.

Chartreuse A distinctively colored green or yellow herbal liqueur with anise notes.

Cognac Brandy made in the Cognac region of France.

Cointreau A bittersweet brandy-based orange liqueur made in France.

Crème de violette Violet liqueur.

Curaçao A generic, sweet orange liqueur made from the peels of the bitter orange native to the island of the same name.

Elisir M.P. Roux A French herbal liqueur that's lightly sweet and floral.

Extra dry Medium dry.

Farigoule A French liqueur flavored with thyme and other herbs and spices.

Ice, cracked To make cracked ice, wrap ice cubes in a clean dish towel and smash them on a hard surface, or hit them with a mallet.

Ice, crushed To make crushed ice, grind ice cubes in a high-powered blender or ice crusher. The crushed ice made by refrigerator ice makers, or sometimes available in bags at grocery stores, can also be used.

Lillet An herbal aperitif wine used in cocktails; similar to vermouth.

Limoncello A sweet, tart, bright yellow lemon liqueur.

Lychee A round, sweet, red-shelled fruit, with translucent white flesh, native to Asia.

Maraschino liqueur A clear cherry liqueur with almond notes. Made in Italy with Marasca cherries.

Moscato d'Asti A sweet, mildly sparkling Italian wine made from the Muscat grape.

Muddle To bruise ingredients with a muddler (a rod with a flattened end), or a spoon.

Muscat A sweet, floral wine grape used to make Asti, Moscato d'Asti, and some ice wines.

Orange bitters Bitters flavored in part with orange zest, such as Regan's Orange Bitters No. 6, and Fee Brothers Orange Bitters.

Orgeat A syrup flavored with almond and other flavors including orange flower water.

Pastis Anise-flavored liqueur.

Peach bitters Bitters flavored in part with peach, such as Fee Brothers Peach Bitters.

Pernod A French brand of pastis.

Peychaud's bitters A proprietary bitters formula that originated in New Orleans in 1793.

Prosecco A moderately sparkling Italian wine with a supple body and hints of apple and peach.

Real maraschino cherries Marasca cherries packed in a thick maraschino liqueur syrup, typically imported from Italy, such as those made by Luxardo. Can also refer to other artisan-made cocktail cherries packed in a thick syrup of maraschino liqueur and not chemically processed.

Sekt A fully sparkling German wine often made from Riesling grapes.

Simple syrup A common sugar syrup, typically used to sweeten liquids because it dissolves easily. Make it at home by combining equal parts raw sugar and boiling water until the sugar is dissolved. Refrigerate, covered tightly, for up to 2 weeks, then discard. (For a product that will keep indefinitely, add 1 ounce of vodka for every 2 cups of simple syrup.)

Sparkling red Lightly sparkling red wine, usually from Australia, such as sparkling Shiraz and Cabernet, or Italy, such as sparkling Lambrusco.

Sparkling rosé A pink wine that usually gets its color from red grapes with the skins left on.

Sparkling sake A mildly sparkling fermented rice drink from Japan, with a milky white color.

Sparkling wine In this book, Champagne-style sparklers made outside the Champagne region: in California and other U.S. states; France, Australia, New Zealand, South Africa, Chile, Argentina, Canada, and, increasingly, other parts of the world.

St. Germain Aromatic elderflower liqueur made in France by U.S.-based Cooper Spirits.

Twist The classic cocktail garnish, a twist is a short strip of citrus peel commonly carved from the skin of the fruit using a special tool called a channel knife, or cut to size from larger pieces of peel sliced off with a paring knife. (Only use the colored portion of the peel, where the oils reside, not the bitter white pith beneath.) The citrus strip is usually twisted over a drink to release the flavorful oils and add flavor, and then dropped into the liquid to add color.

| RESOURCE GUIDE |

ALCOHOL-FREE SPARKLERS:

Dry Soda, drysoda.com

Vignette Wine Country Soda, winecountrysoda.com

Sweetwater Cellars Sparkling Grape Juices and Ciders, sweetwatercellars.com

BITTERS:

Angostura, angostura.com

Peychaud's, sazerac.com

Fee Brothers (for peach bitters, orange bitters, and others), feebrothers.com

Regan's Orange Bitters No. 6, buffalotrace.com

BLENDERS AND ICE CRUSHERS:

Blendtec blenders, blendtec.com

Vita-Mix blenders, vitamix.com

Metrokane ice crushers, metrokane.com

BOTTLE OPENERS:

Screwpull Cork Catcher, screwpull.com

Metrokane Velvet Champagne Pliers, metrokane.com

CHAMPAGNE SAVERS:

Vacuvin Champagne Saver, vacuvin.nl

Argyle Champagne Stopper, argylewineaccessories.com.au

Sur La Table Champagne Stopper, surlatable.com

GLASSWARE:

Reproduction Stork Club saucers, newyorkfirst.com

Saucers and flutes, crateandbarrel.com and macys.com

REAL MARASCHINO CHERRIES:

Luxardo cherries, preissimports.com

Toschi amarena cherries, europantry.com

SPARKLING WINES:

Affordable single bottles and cases, traderjoes.com (in stores only)

Large selection, wallywine.com and wine.com

Sparkling sake, truesake.com

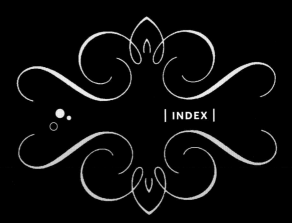

| INDEX |

LIQUID MEASUREMENTS

Bar spoon = ½ ounce

1 teaspoon = ⅙ ounce

1 tablespoon = ½ ounce

2 tablespoons (pony) = 1 ounce

3 tablespoons (jigger) = 1½ ounces

¼ cup = 2 ounces

⅓ cup = 3 ounces

½ cup = 4 ounces

⅔ cup = 5 ounces

¾ cup = 6 ounces

1 cup = 8 ounces

1 pint = 16 ounces

1 quart = 32 ounces

750-ml bottle = 25.4 ounces

1-liter bottle = 33.8 ounces

1 medium lemon = 3 tablespoons juice

1 medium lime = 2 tablespoons juice

1 medium orange = ⅓ cup juice

TABLE OF EQUIVALENTS

The exact equivalents in the following tables have been rounded for convenience.

LIQUID/DRY MEASUREMENTS

U.S.	METRIC
¼ teaspoon	1.25 milliliters
½ teaspoon	2.5 milliliters
1 teaspoon	5 milliliters
1 tablespoon (3 teaspoons)	15 milliliters
1 fluid ounce (2 tablespoons)	30 milliliters
¼ cup	60 milliliters
⅓ cup	80 milliliters
½ cup	120 milliliters
1 cup	240 milliliters
1 pint (2 cups)	480 milliliters
1 quart (4 cups, 32 ounces)	960 milliliters
1 gallon (4 quarts)	3.84 liters
1 ounce (by weight)	28 grams
1 pound	448 grams
2.2 pounds	1 kilogram

LENGTHS

U.S.	METRIC
⅛ inch	3 millimeters
¼ inch	6 millimeters
½ inch	12 millimeters
1 inch	2.5 centimeters

OVEN TEMPERATURES

FAHRENHEIT	CELSIUS	GAS
250	120	½
275	140	1
300	150	2
325	160	3
350	180	4
375	190	5
400	200	6
425	220	7
450	230	8
475	240	9
500	260	10

Pop!